YOU
ARE NOT ALONE

MADELINE GANDY

ISBN 979-8-88616-875-4 (paperback)
ISBN 979-8-88832-236-9 (hardcover)
ISBN 979-8-88616-876-1 (digital)

Christian Faith Publishing
832 Park Avenue
Meadville, PA 16335
www.christianfaithpublishing.com

Printed in the United States of America

To my loving husband Nate and my three beautiful
kids Elijah, Aaliyah, and Imani, with love.

Often, we go through life not realizing the impact we have on those around us. Have you ever said to yourself, "What memory do I want to leave behind? Or what kind of impact do I want to have on people?" An important thing to keep in mind is that no one is perfect. We all make mistakes in life, but how we respond to our failures or our mess-ups in life is what is crucial to our daily walk with the Lord. What kind of example can we set for those who are watching us? We can impact people by our words and even by our actions. Let your light shine and allow the Holy Spirit to use you to inspire those around you.

> Let your light so shine before men, that they may see your good works and glorify your Father in heaven (Matthew 5:16 NKJV).

spiritual mindfulness UNCONDITIONAL
expression SOUL kindness FEEL joy
awareness HEART just be LOVE attitude
intention blessings
integrity oneness
compassion gratitude NOW
pure GRACE choice
PURPOSE faith
HEALING perspective

Let us be optimistic, not pessimistic. Optimism brings strength, and pessimism just beats you down, which in the long run brings defeat. Try to go through life with a positive attitude, and thank God for the little things. Focusing on the negative just causes us to lose sight of the blessings that Jesus has already placed in front of us. If you woke up to see another day, can walk, talk, breathe, see, feel, etc., give Him thanks. Today, I thank God for His never-ending love, my family, my health, and for the Lord's constant provision. What do you thank God for today?

> Oh, give thanks to the Lord, for He is good! For His mercy endures forever (Psalm 118:29 NKJV).

God is good all the time. Through the good, the bad, the most challenging times, and just the okay days. I challenge you to be grateful for what He's brought you through. Be grateful for what He's carrying you through and be grateful for where He is leading you. Rejoice in the Lord in every season of your life because in those moments of rejoicing, during those most difficult times in your life, your problem begins to become so much smaller compared to the great and Almighty God that we serve. The same God who created heaven and the earth. Remember, He has already won the battle. Don't hold back from rejoicing in advance. Again, I repeat, the battle has already been won. Rejoice in the Lord, for He is so good.

Rejoice in the Lord always. Again, I will say, rejoice! (Philippians 4:4 NKJV).

Rest in the Lord. He is your strength. He is your rock during your most trying times and carrying you through. You are an overcomer. Many times, these are the exact words we have to constantly repeat in our heads till we truly believe it and walk it out. This is God's word to us, and His word will set you free. As you may have heard before, "The truth will set you free." Well, this is indeed true because God's Word breathes life and continues to set captives free today. Meditate daily on His Word, the Bread of Life, and you will receive freedom in Christ Jesus.

Now the Lord is the Spirit; and where the Spirit of the Lord is, there is liberty (2 Corinthians 3:17 NKJV).

closed

A closed door may not feel good at times, but always remember it may be a blessing in disguise.

I have experienced this blessing in disguise. It all started with my intent to pursue a different position at my place of employment. I made multiple attempts to get an interview each time the posting came up. I even went to the length of reaching out to the supervisor to seek advice as to what I could do to work toward the goal of getting this position. Oddly enough, I received no response, and with each attempt I made, it was unsuccessful. The more I knocked on that door, the more frustrated I became when that door would not open. At that moment, it dawned on me that with my experience with other closed doors over the years that in some cases, it may just be that it is not meant for me to walk through that door. That door was shut for a reason.

After a week or so, my coworker reached out to see how I made out with the application/interview process. As I shared with her my experience, she went on to say, regarding the position that I had applied for, that it was basically demanding and came with high stress, which was leading to a quick turnaround. Those who got the position would end up leaving. The closed door did not feel good for sure, but what feels even better is knowing that the Lord always looks out for His children. The Lord blocked that transfer for a reason, and that alone shows how much He cares for us. He is our protector and forever our strong tower.

> As for God, His way is perfect; The word of the Lord is proven; He is a shield to all who trust in Him (Psalm 18:30 NKJV).

PRAYER AND
JOURNAL PAGE

Breathe

DAY 6

Do not let what you can't control, control you. Let go, let God, and simply breathe. We were created to live life more abundantly. How do we live an abundant life? By knowing the God we serve is concerned about every detail of our lives and will work out everything for good for those who love Him and are called according to His purpose. God is with you. You are not alone. If God is for you, then who can be against you? Cast every concern, worry, fear, and anxious thought unto the Lord and experience His peace today.

> The thief does not come except to steal, and to kill, and to destroy. I have come that they may have life, and that they may have it more abundantly (John 10:10 NKJV).

Some time ago, I saw a post on Facebook that captured my attention. It showed this woman going through many obstacle courses during a competition. This woman in the video showed so much agility and endurance. As difficult as the obstacles appeared to be, she fought through it with a goal in mind. That goal was to win. It made me think about how this mentality can be applied to our walk with the Lord. The same way she endured these obstacles is the same way we can endure the challenges in our lives. Fight and don't give up. Giving up should never ever be an option. Throughout all the chaos that life brings, it is tempting to just give up, but I encourage to keep your eye on the prize (Jesus), push through, endure, and keep the faith

Therefore we also, since
we are surrounded by so great a
cloud of witnesses, let us lay aside

every weight, and the sin which so easily ensnares us, and let us run with endurance the race that is set before us, looking unto Jesus, the author and finisher of our faith, who for the joy that was set before Him endured the cross, despising the shame, and has sat down at the right hand of the throne of God (Hebrews 12:1–2 NKJV).

PRAYER AND
JOURNAL PAGE

When things get hard or look impossible to the natural eye, it is easy for one to just give up. I think when we are not willing to work at achieving what God has put in our hearts, we are letting go of the blessing that may be right around the corner. It is not always going to be easy, and we may feel the pressure. Anything that we must work so hard for blossoms into something more beautiful than what we can even fathom or imagine. Even diamonds must go through so much pressure before it gets to its beautiful form. Your hard work is not going unnoticed. The Lord sees all. Life can be hard. We are under so much pressure often, but in time, your season of blossoming is coming. Be patient. There is light at the end of that tunnel. Hold on to God's promises.

> Blessed is the man who endures temptation; for when he has been approved, he will receive the crown of life which the Lord has promised to those who love Him (James 1:12 NKJV).

DAY
9

Time spent with Christ—you have nothing to lose but the following: worry, anxiety, depression, fear, anger, past hurt, and more. Once we let go of those things that we tend to allow to stress us and keep us in a state of defeat, we, in turn, begin to bear fruit (love, joy, peace, forbearance, kindness, goodness, faithfulness, gentleness and self-control). Be ready to walk in the peace of God that surpasses all understanding and unexplainable joy. Time spent with Christ leads to VICTORY.

> Abide in Me, and I in you. As the branch cannot bear fruit of itself, unless it abides in the vine, neither can you, unless you abide in Me.
>
> I am the vine, you are the branches. He who abides in Me, and I in him, bears much fruit; for without Me you can do nothing (John 15:4–5 NKJV).

Many times, I have questioned what my purpose or calling was. It's so easy for us to compare ourselves to others based on others' natural talents or gifts. We must remember that we are all not built the same. Or maybe you feel that you get overlooked because you are different or your lack of an ability or gift. We must remember that God does not call the qualified, but He qualifies the called. There are many examples in the Bible where God used people who we may look at today as not being qualified, but they were exactly who God was looking for. He knew the heart.

I know I'm not the best speaker or gifted as others may be, but I know I can't allow that to paralyze me. I know the Lord has more for me. Don't let your fears or lack of cause you to miss out on your calling. In our weakness, He is made stronger. Keep pushing through and seek the Lord for direction and His calling on your life. It's amazing what the Lord can do through us.

> And He said to me, 'My grace is sufficient for you, for My strength is made perfect in weakness.' Therefore, most gladly I will rather boast in my infirmities, that the power of Christ may rest upon me (2 Corinthians 12:9 NKJV).

PRAYER AND
JOURNAL PAGE

The Lord provides lessons daily, and I am so grateful for it. He uses many things to speak to us and guide us. What the Lord continues to bring to my mind is perseverance. This weekend after my daughter's basketball games, I gave her the talk—what she did great in and what she needs to work on. She doesn't like these talks, but it will only benefit her in the long run. My main points with her were to continue to push through, fight, and don't give up. With time and continual practice, those areas that need improvement will no longer be an obstacle. Those obstacles are providing her with many lessons that she can either choose to grow from or she can do nothing about and allow it to remain a barrier. I see how much she wants to do well.

This also applies to our walk in life, our walk with God. Perseverance is pushing forward despite whatever obstacle is thrown your way. We all have shortcomings or mistakes that we make. It's how we respond to them that matters. Do we wallow in self-pity and say woe is me and just give up? Or do we pick ourselves up and continue to push through them? My reliance on God is what gives me strength and hope each day. Remember, perseverance produces character. Today, eliminate failure, hopelessness, not good enough from your mind and speech and, instead, continue to push through and say,

"I can do all things through Christ who strengthens me" (Philippians 4:13 NKJV).

PRAYER AND
JOURNAL PAGE

You, too, can walk on water if you keep your gaze upon the Lord. It's when you remove your eyes off Him that you begin to sink. Stay above the water. Keep your eyes on the prize, and He will see you through.

And Peter answered Him and said, "Lord, if it is You, command me to come to You on the water." So He said, "Come." And when Peter had come down out of the boat, he walked on the water to go to Jesus. But when he saw that the wind was boisterous, he was afraid; and beginning to sink he cried out, saying, "Lord, save me!" And immediately Jesus stretched out His hand and caught him, and said to him, "O you of little faith, why did you doubt?" And when they got into the boat, the wind ceased (Matthew 14:28–33 NKJV).

While we are going through the process, we must remain faithful to our Lord knowing that we are going through a state of pruning and molding. The Lord is preparing us for wherever He is leading us to. Our old state of thinking, our insecurities, or maybe lack of empathy, etc. is not allowed to come with us, so we must go through the fire before we get to the next level. Keep in mind that we are not in the fire alone. He is right beside us. The Lord is not surprised one bit by what we are facing at this time. He knew we would be here. He is all-knowing. He loves us so much that He gave us the tools to utilize throughout the process.

We must keep fighting; we must keep pushing through knowing that in our weaknesses, He is made strong. Fast and pray if you must. Matter of fact, I encourage you to. Remember, He will never leave us nor forsake us, and He will never give us more than we can handle. He remains faithful and mighty in power. Because He is God, our Mighty Counselor, our Prince of Peace, the Lord of lords. There is nothing more powerful than the God we serve. Not even the process because God is sovereign and will always be.

> Every branch in Me that
> does not bear fruit He takes away;
> and every branch that bears fruit
> He prunes, that it may bear more
> fruit (John 15:2 NKJV).

PRAYER AND
JOURNAL PAGE

Have you ever chosen to take a shortcut in your travels only to find out that it had major delays due to all the traffic headed in the same direction? Had you stayed on the previous route, you would have made it to your destination sooner. Your breakthrough or that answered prayer may seem to be taking eternity, but keep forging through. Do not try to take shortcuts. It could lead to LONGER delays. What may seem like a shortcut may end up being a longer route. Remain on the narrow path. It is not an easy path for most, but there is a great reward to those who endure it.

The Narrow Way—'Enter by the narrow gate; for wide is the gate and broad is the way that leads to destruction, and there are many who go in by it. Because narrow is the gate and difficult is the way which leads to life, and there are few who find it' (Matthew 7:13–14 NKJV).

Distractions are meant to pull you away or delay you from reaching the mark. Distractions can be detrimental. It is like cooking, which requires focus. I am sure many of us have done this when we are cooking. We get distracted by a phone call, TV show, etc. Our focus has been removed from our cooking and on to something else. As our focus remains on that something else, our food begins to overcook, which eventually burns, becoming no longer edible. It is useless for its main purpose of nourishment. Had we remained focused on that meal, it would have served its purpose.

However, there still is hope. Good thing is we can try again. But this time, put all your focus on that meal, and the results will be wonderful. Well, it will not be burned at least. What is distracting you today? Has it removed your eyes off the cross? Fix your eyes solely on Jesus. Once your eyes are on the One above, the results will be amazing.

> Set your mind on things above, not on things on the earth (Colossians 3:2 NKJV).

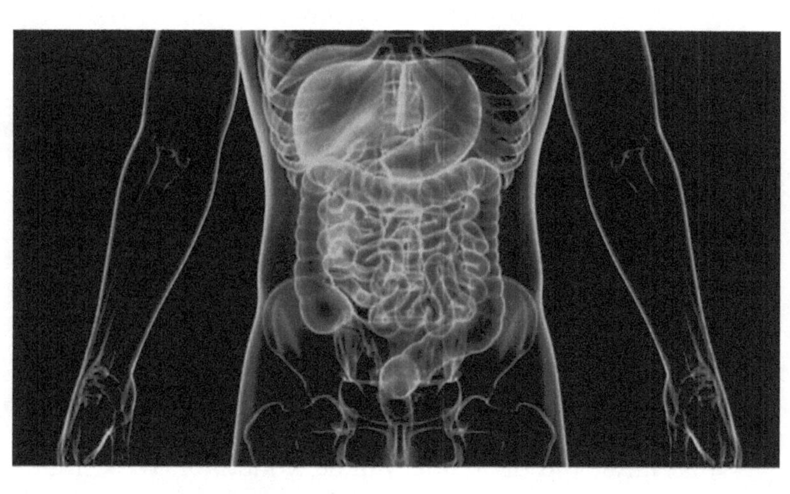

There is no way that there is not a God. Consider the details of the human body. Many of its functions are complex. That alone shows me how passionate and detailed God is with His creation. Or even take the clouds in the sky, which always seem to amaze me. The beauty that it captures and displays, I am always in awe because He created that beauty for us. It is similar to an artist and their masterpiece. An artist is very detailed and passionate while creating their masterpiece. We are all a creation of something far more superior than an explosion such as the big bang theory or from evolution. I refuse to believe that our existence is accidental. We have a purpose. We are a masterpiece made from the hand of God. We are fearfully and wonderfully created.

I will praise You, for I am
fearfully and wonderfully made;
Marvelous are Your works, And
that my soul knows very well
(Psalm 139:14 NKJV).

My heart breaks for this nation. My heart breaks for injustice. My heart breaks for racism. My heart breaks for division. Seeking the Lord even more in these dark times has given me hope in my heart. The Lord reminds me His love is beyond our comprehension. The sacrifice He made for us on the cross, the unconditional love He has for us, even when we have turned our backs on Him. But He continues to forgive us each time with opened arms. That is real love. In these dark times, the Lord has reminded me that I must continue to love. We must love because He first loved us. Just imagine if we all had the love of Christ in our hearts. Our nation would be in such a different place. Jesus is the only answer because He is love. Let God's love and hope prevail in your heart today.

Love is patient, love is kind. It does not envy, it does not boast, it is not proud. It does not dishonor others, it is not self-seeking, it is not easily angered, it keeps no record of wrongs. Love does not delight in evil but rejoices with the truth. It always protects, always trusts, always hopes, always perseveres. Love never fails (1 Corinthians 13:4–8 NIV).

PRAYER AND JOURNAL PAGE

Deep thoughts: As I am sitting here, I'm thinking of how different I feel I am from many people. I can be very socially awkward, quiet, and shy around people (unless I really know you). I do find it very frustrating. Sometimes when I speak out loud, the words don't come out exactly the way it was articulated in my mind. I have cried over this. I have even asked the Lord why He made me this way along with why do I feel as if I am so different? Why can't I be like this person or that person? I have even prayed for Him to change me so I can be a better speaker, outspoken, etc. But, weirdly enough, now I'm not sure if I really want that prayer answered. I have come to realize that during those moments of vulnerability, I really rely on Jesus that I look to Him to strengthen me, guide me, lead me, and speak through me as He sees fit. I had to remember that, even in our limitations, the Lord moves on our behalf, and He is glorified through it all. The Lord reminded me of Moses and his speech impediment. With the Lord knowing of Moses's defect, he still chose to use him.

What if I was the best speaker? Would I completely rely on Him as much? Or would I become so confident in myself and in my own abilities, pushing Him to the back burner? Would I become overconfident? What if I had all the money in the world? Would I use it wisely and help many in need? Or would I self-indulge in materialistic things? It is easy to say what I think I would do, but once it's a reality, sometimes, it's a different story.

I do not want to ever put anything before the God for whom saw me worth dying for. My reliance is solely on Christ, and I am okay with that. He is molding and sculpting an imperfect person who not only relies on Him but is learning to fully trust Him in all things. Remember, remain humble in all things. Don't allow pride to creep in, which takes the focus off Jesus and on self. Anything that we can do/accomplish or have accomplished in our life is only by the grace of God.

> But one and the same Spirit
> works all these things, distributing
> to each one individually as He wills
> (1 Corinthians 12:11 NKJV).

And He said to me, "My grace is sufficient for you, for My strength is made perfect in weakness." Therefore most gladly I will rather boast in my infirmities, that the power of Christ may rest upon me (2 Corinthians 12:9 NKJV.)

It is easy for one to get entangled in the web of lies that the enemy offers. Being so caught up in the mainstream can dim one's focus. Regain focus (twenty-twenty vision) and get caught up in God's Word today. Stay in God's Word daily to show yourself approved (2 Timothy 2:15). To walk into a battle unarmored is foolish, so why do we walk into a spiritual battle without first suiting up daily with the armor of God? Be wise and suit up not only when we feel like it but at all times. As we all have heard before, poor preparation produces poor performance. If you are not prepared for the battle, your performance will be poor. You are opening yourself up to becoming an easy target. We must put on our armor daily and fight the great fight. You are victorious.

Finally, my brethren, be strong in the Lord and in the power of His might. Put on the whole armor of God, that you may be able to stand against the wiles of the devil. For we do not wrestle against flesh and blood, but against principalities, against powers, against the rulers of the darkness of this age, against spiritual hosts of wickedness in the heavenly places. Therefore take up the whole armor of God, that you may be able to withstand in the evil day, and having done all, to stand (Ephesians 6:10–13 NKJV).

PRAYER AND
JOURNAL PAGE

Have you ever sought an item you lost? That item that is so priceless to you? Maybe an item such as an heirloom that was so dear to your family? You were so determined to find it. So diligent in your searching. You've searched for it with all your heart and strength. If only you could just find that priceless item, how satisfied you would be. The joy that it would bring to your heart or even the peace that you would receive. The same way you sought that item, put that same strength in searching for God. Be relentless in your seeking, and you will find Him.

And you will seek Me and find Me when you search for Me with all your heart (Jeremiah 29:13 NKJV).

But without faith it is impossible to please him: for

he that cometh to God must
believe that he is, and that he is a
rewarder of them that diligently
seek him (Hebrews 11:6 KJV).

PRAYER AND
JOURNAL PAGE

There's a difference between knowing God and truly knowing Him. To know is to spend time with Him. Continue to sit at Jesus's feet. The more you sit at His feet, the more you are in tune with His true character and His voice. I know many people, but it doesn't mean I really know them or know who they are. I may happen to know a few of their likes and dislikes, but I cannot say that I really know them. Maybe you're one who has many followers on your social media accounts; you know who they are from work or maybe through another friend. You consider them more as an acquaintance, but can you say that you really know them, if you don't invest any time in getting to know them? The best investment that you can ever make in your lifetime, is investing your time in Jesus.

Draw near to God, and He
will draw near to you (James 4:8
NKJV).

Jesus

There are many terrible things occurring throughout this nation/this world. As we all know, racial injustice, COVID-19, child/human trafficking, and many more have plagued this earth. But the Lord reminded me of this; that there is something far more severe than these. The greatest pandemic of them all. That pandemic: Many falling away, many turning to other gods/idols, many not coming to know Christ. Once God is removed, all hell breaks loose. Just think about it for a minute. A world that puts Jesus first in everything is a world in unity, a world of peace. Jesus is love. Jesus brings hope. He brings peace to those who are willing to receive Him. He sets captives free. He brings forgiveness. He brings healing and restoration.

My prayer is for all to come to know Christ. That many will have their life-changing aha moment with the Lord. A personal experience that will only point to Jesus. Jesus is alive. Don't let me convince you. Seek Him today and experience His love, and may your hope be restored.

> Blessed is the man who trusts in the Lord, and whose hope is the Lord (Jeremiah 17:7 NKJV).

PRAYER AND
JOURNAL PAGE

One morning, after eating a bowl of cereal, I headed to the sink to rinse out my bowl. Instead of dumping out the rest of the milk that was left in my bowl, I found myself turning on the water and just watched as the bowl of milk was being filled with water. As I continued to watch, the water began to overflow the bowl. I then began to see what was once a bowl full of milk, now becoming clearer and clearer. Now it was a bowl of clear water with no sign of milk anymore.

The Lord showed me this: Our transformation is like this bowl of milk. The running water is the living water. Jesus Christ's living word. Milk symbolizes us, our sinful cloudy nature. When you allow the living water (God's Word) to continuously flow in your life, there will eventually be clear evidence of your transformation. Keep in mind that there will be a process of pruning and refining, but as you consistently seek Him and drink of the living water, transformation continues to occur in you. Even if you may not see it right away, things are continuing to be chipped away. Turning up the water is when we give full control to the Lord. Transformation from milk to water takes place much quicker.

However, if you let the water flow at a very slow pace in the milk, the transformation may take much longer. This slow running of the water symbolizes the lack of control we give to the Lord. Trying to do it on our own, not being consistent in our walk, holding back because of fear, doubting God, and not moving forward because of our lack of faith, and not seeking Him. Don't lose hope. Everyone's journey is different from one another. Continue to drink of the living water and allow His transformation to change you from the inside out.

> But whoever drinks of the water that I shall give him will never thirst. But the water that I shall give him will become in him a fountain of water springing up into everlasting life (John 4:14 NKJV).

PRAYER AND JOURNAL PAGE

Dream: In my dream, I was driving down a familiar street, and I happened to look to my right in an empty parking lot. In that parking lot, I see a car full of people, chained up in shackles, resembling slaves. As I see this, I begin to look around in shock that no one is bothered by this. In my mind, I am asking, *Where is the outcry? This is inhumane.*

Once I awoke, I automatically knew that the Lord wanted to share something with me. What He shared was this: those who were in shackles are many who are bounded by sin. They have allowed the shackles and chains to become a norm for them. They are bounded but are okay with it, not realizing that it is leading to their demise.

We are not meant to be bounded. Don't normalize the struggle. Seek the Lord for breakthrough. Keep fighting and persevere.

> Let us not become weary in
> doing good, for at the proper time
> we will reap a harvest if we do not
> give up (Galatians 6:9 NIV).

Let these words of Jesus sink in this morning:

When everything around you seems to be going wrong, when circumstances seem impossible, when that miracle has not yet come to fruition, even when you are asleep at night, He is still working. Continue to hold on to His every promise. There is light in what may seem to be a long dark tunnel. Trust and believe that the Lord will see you through. Remember, His ways are not our ways, and His timing is not our timing, but He always shows up on time. You can't see all that He is doing, but know He is working on your behalf.

> My Father is always at his work to this very day, and I too am working (John 5:17 NIV).

Good intentions do not equal obedience. Good intentions can be an act of disobedience if it's apart from obedience to God. In other words, are you walking in God's will or in your own will? It may sound like a good idea, but is it what the Lord has called you to do? Lord, help us to walk in your will as we abide in you and be obedient to do whatever you are calling us to do. Not our will but your will be done.

> If you abide in Me, and My words abide in you, you[a] will ask what you desire, and it shall be done for you (John 15:7 NKJV).

> Behold, to obey is better than sacrifice (1 Samuel 15:22 NKJV).

Dream: So let me tell you about this weird dream that I had this morning. In my dream, this stranger came into my home, mistaking it as her own home. After making her realize that this was my home, I opened the door to let her out. At the end of this dream, I see that she is in my home again. I'm on the outside this time, but I hear her banging on the door, trying to get out. I'm standing there watching and not understanding why she is having so much trouble opening this door when the door is working perfectly fine. I remember this door that she was banging on being orange. Of course, when I woke up, I was thinking, *This dream is odd. Could this be a dream reminding me that I need my doorknobs replaced?* Lol.

So I was wondering why the door was orange. I researched what orange symbolizes in the Bible, and this is what I found: orange symbolizes endurance and strength. But I began to ask the Lord, "What are you trying to show me? I'm listening."

This is what I heard: Some of you are in your own prison. Imprisoned in your own mind, imprisoned by your own thoughts. You have been banging on that door in hopes of someone setting you free. You have the lock on your side of the door, a functioning doorknob, a movable and unblocked door, but you are continuing to have challenges opening that door. All you must do is unlock that door, turn that doorknob, push on the door, and walk right through it.

But your judgment, your vision, has been clouded making it very difficult for you to see what's right in front of you. In some ways, you have allowed the enemy to set up residency in your mind, which gives him freedom to set up barricades in front of a perfectly cleared exit. Allowing the enemy to interfere with the way you think, move, and act. You're trapped, so you think at least. If only you can see the clear exit in front of you. Jesus offers freedom in Him. Seek Him for freedom. He is truly for freedom. He is truly the only answer.

My prayer: Lord, help us to see through your lens. Set us free from old mindsets. Mindsets of confusion and twisted perception. Give us clarity. A mind full of God-breathed truth and not what this world defines as truth because your truth, your power, your strength is what sets us free. Negative thinking—you need to go, and we release you from us. Fear—you must leave. We kick you to the curb. As we unlock that door, turn that doorknob, and push on that door. Lord, give us the courage to take that step to walk right through and endure to the end.

> Stand fast therefore in the liberty by which Christ has made us free, and do not be entangled again with a yoke of bondage (Galatians 5:1).

> Now the Lord is the Spirit; and where the Spirit of the Lord is, there is liberty (2 Corinthians 3:17).

The Lord is speaking. Be still and be quiet long enough to listen, and you will hear. You can't hear what one is speaking if your mouth is constantly moving, if you are listening to the wrong voices, or your mind is elsewhere. That also applies when you're trying to hear from the Lord. Be still and listen for the voice of God.

> Be still and know that I am God (Psalm 46:10 NKJV).

> Give ear and hear my voice, Listen and hear my speech (Isaiah 28:23 NKJV).

> But He said, "More than that, blessed are those who hear the word of God and keep it!" (Luke 11:28 NKJV).

Son of God. Tha[t]
with God, and ar[e]
us.

God is love. If w[e]
ers, we will stay [with]
God, and he will [stay in us.]
we truly love oth[ers.]

The only love that is consistent is God's agape love. People will come and go, but God will NEVER leave you nor forsake you. His love is limitless. A love that doesn't disappoint. Open your heart today and allow Jesus in. He's waiting with open arms.

> Oh, give thanks to the LORD, for He is good! For His love endures forever (Psalm 136:1 NKJV).

> But God demonstrates His own love toward us, in that while we were still sinners, Christ died for us (Romans 5:8 NKJV).

> Now may the Lord direct your hearts into the love of God and into the patience of Christ (2 Thessalonians 3:5 NKJV).

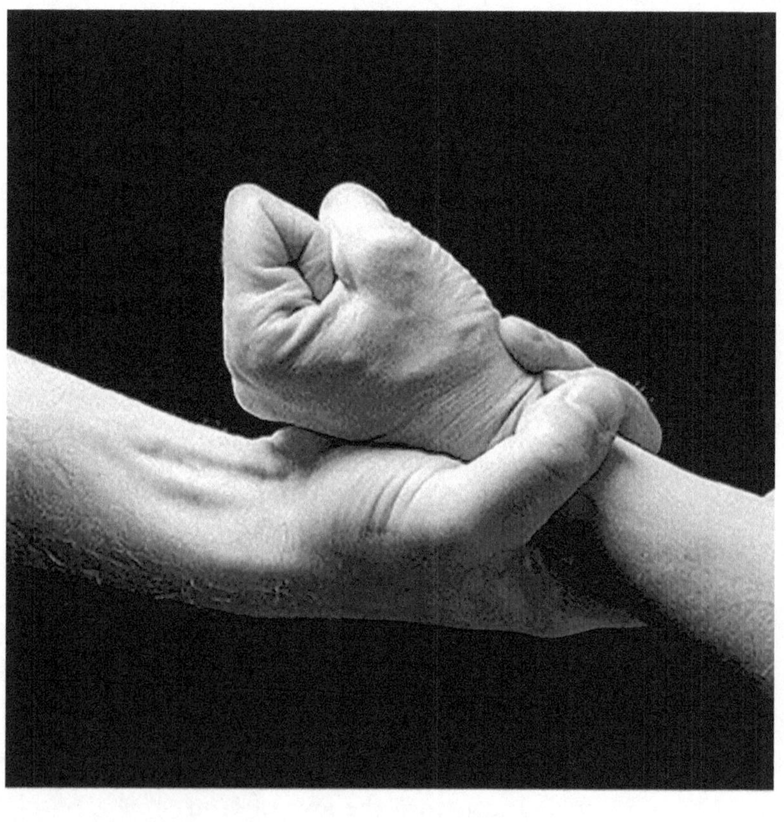

Some of you have been allowing that person, that thing, to steal your joy for far too long now. In some ways, it has become your stumbling block. That peace you once knew seems to be something from the past. It's time to let it go. Forgiveness needs to take place. If you feel like you can't forgive or you can't move on without going back to that moment of hurt and pain (which keeps you from moving forward), give it to God. I promise you, once you do, peace will come. Cast all your burdens on the Lord. The weight you have been carrying will be uplifted. We serve a God of healing and restoration. Once again, let it go. Continuing to hold on to what causes you to lose your peace causes more damage than just letting go.

Therefore humble yourselves under the mighty hand of God, that He may exalt you in due time, casting all your care upon Him, for He cares for you (1 Peter 5:6–7 NKJV).

GOD
IS GOOD
all the
TIME

Regardless of your circumstances in life, think on the goodness of God. His goodness will always give you a whole new perspective of your situation. Remember, God is always so good. His goodness outweighs every trial we face.

> The LORD *is* good, A stronghold in the day of trouble; And He knows those who trust in Him (Nahum 1:7 NKJV).

> To declare that the Lord is upright; He is my rock, and there is no unrighteousness in Him (Psalm 92:15 NKJV).

Open the Word of God. There is so much treasure to be found in it. The more and more you search through His Word, the more He reveals to you.

> Again, the kingdom of heaven is like treasure hidden in a field, which a man found and hid; and for joy over it he goes and sells all that he has and buys that field (Matthew 13:44 NKJV).

> Happy is the man who finds wisdom, And the man who gains understanding; For her proceeds are better than the profits of silver, And her gain than fine gold. She is more precious than rubies, And all the things you may desire cannot compare with her (Proverbs 3:13–15 NKJV).

I think we all have heard a worship song at some point that just spoke to our spirit. One of those songs that is worth listening to on repeat. I'm sure we all can agree that we have enough noise and distraction going on in the world, enough to steal one's peace. Praise and worship do wonders. I know, for me, it gives me joy, hope, and peace because as I worship, I am giving praise to the One who holds my future in His hands. The One who brings hope to the hopeless. The One who heals and restores. The One who loves with a greater love that could never disappoint. The One who thought I was worth dying for. That One is Jesus.

So I will bless You as long as
I live; in Your name I will lift up
my hands (Psalm 63:4 ESV).

The Lord put a song of praise in my heart this morning. As I was humming and thinking on the words, I began to think to myself what a disservice we do to ourselves when we don't lift Him up in praise. As the praises go up, the blessings come down. Blessings of joy, hope, etc. Why wouldn't we want to sing praises, knowing this power that exists in what we speak or even sing? You are speaking life when you praise and worship the Lord. Give praise to the Almighty today.

Death and life *are* in the power of the tongue, And those who love it will eat its fruit (Proverbs 18:21 NKJV).

Let my mouth be filled with Your praise And with Your glory all the day (Psalm 71:8 NKJV).

Remember, always seek a lesson or a word from the Lord in every moment. He could be revealing something to you today. Just take the time to listen. This is what the Lord showed me: Don't easily give in when facing opposition/under pressure for your faith in Christ. Hold on to God's Word, even if you must stand alone. We must ask ourselves if we are facing opposition, what will our response be? How would we react? Would we hold on strong to God's Word? Or will we give in so easily? Will you stand firm on His Word, even if it's not within the popular vote? Will you remain faithful, even if the world says otherwise? Remember, even though you may feel like you are at it alone, He remains at your side. Just continue to fight the good fight. Those who endure will finish strong.

> Therefore, my beloved brethren, be steadfast, immovable, always abounding in the work of the Lord, knowing that your labor is not in vain in the Lord (1 Corinthians 15:58 NKJV).

FALSE
TRUE

Here's a question for you. Have you ever been lied to? I'm sure many of us can say we have. It's not a good feeling to be lied to. You get to a point of just not believing anything that person says anymore because there is this doubt in your mind that anything flowing from their mouth is facts. Many times, we lose complete trust in them. We can all agree that there is one who is well-known for this. That one would be the enemy who is the father of all lies.

Just as you would stop believing that person or cut them off due to their lies, it's time we stop believing the lies of the enemy. Some of us have been believing the lies of the enemy for far too long, and it's time to cut him right off. Renounce those lies right now. Whatever lie(s) you have believed over the years about yourself, replace them with God's truth. Begin to believe in the truth. Speak the truth out loud. Remember, Jesus is the truth. Meditate on Jesus's truth and hold on to His every promise.

> Finally, brethren, whatever things are true, whatever things are noble, whatever things are just, whatever things are pure, whatever things are lovely, whatever things are of good report, if there is any virtue and if there is anything praiseworthy—meditate on these things (Philippians 4:8 NKJV).

PRAYER AND JOURNAL PAGE

Priority #1

Priority #2

Priority #3

How many of us get so busy in life that somehow, we get to the point where we find ourselves pushing God to the back burner? Amid the busyness, that alone time with Jesus begins to not be as important as the doing. I know for me, I begin to feel the effects of it when I stop making Jesus the priority. It begins to flow in my attitude and how I carry myself, allowing my old self to try to creep back in. The light that once burned so bright within starts to become dim. Peace tends to slip away while anxiety, hopelessness, and frustration attempt to take their place. Jesus is a necessity regardless of how busy life gets. He is the air we breathe. He is that high-flow oxygen required for us to sustain life.

We can't see Him physically, but we know He is there, and we need Him to survive. Or even like food that provides us with the fuel needed to function, to move, to think, Jesus is needed for us to move in the right direction, think with the mind of Christ, and function in this world. Without Him, we open ourselves up to be vulnerable to fleshly desires. Prioritize Jesus and regain that peace that only He can provide. Don't get caught up in the doing and miss out on the blessing.

Now it happened as they went that He entered a certain village; and a certain woman named Martha welcomed Him into her house. And she had a sister called Mary, who also sat at Jesus' feet and heard His word. But Martha was distracted with much serving, and she approached Him and said, "Lord, do You not care that my sister has left me to serve alone? Therefore, tell her to help me. And Jesus answered and said to her, "Martha, Martha, you are worried and troubled about many things. But one thing is needed, and Mary has chosen that good part, which will not be taken away from her" (Luke 10:38–42 NKJV).

In Closing

Did you know that being a good person is not the key to salvation? Wanting to do good/good works follows once you have the mind of Christ, but it's not your ticket or VIP access to His heavenly kingdom. Salvation is a gift from the Lord. If you don't know the Lord and you have never received Him into your heart as your personal Lord and Savior, it's time to receive and to get to know Him. Let today be a day of repentance; a day of deliverance from your old self, made new unto Jesus, our Lord and Savior; and a day of walking away from idols. Let today be a day of healing, restoration, and freedom. Lay everything down at His feet, and allow the Lord to set you free today. There is freedom in Jesus. Matthew 25:13 (NKJV) states, "Watch therefore, for you know neither the day nor the hour in which the Son of Man is coming." He will return in a blink of an eye. Now is the time.

According to God's Word, this is how one can be saved:

For by grace you have been saved through faith, and that not of yourselves; it is the gift of God, not of works, lest anyone should boast (Ephesians 2:8–9 NKJV). Believe on the Lord Jesus and you will be saved (Acts 16:31 NKJV). If you confess with your mouth the Lord Jesus and believe in your heart that God has raised Him from the dead, you will be saved. For with the heart one believes unto righteousness, and with the mouth confession is made unto salvation (Romans 10:9–10 NKJV). And that you put on the new man which was created according to God, in true righteousness and holiness (Ephesians 4:24 NKJV).

FYI, salvation equals repentance—a changed life, freedom in Christ, getting rid of the old, and stepping into the new.

If you just accepted Jesus into your heart as your
Lord and Savior, welcome to new beginnings.

About the Author

Madeline Gandy, born and raised in Upstate New York, is a born-again Christian and has known the Lord since her childhood. She accepted Jesus as her Lord and Savior as a young girl, before hitting her teen years.

As she reached her teen years, some struggles and trying times came along in her life, losing her focus on who she was in the Lord, causing her to stray away. But by the grace of God, in her early thirties, she rededicated her life to the Lord, making every effort to keep pushing through. One word she holds on to from the Holy Bible is perseverance, and that is what her life consists of, persevering in all trials and challenges that life throws at her with Christ as her foundation.

When she could not focus enough to read the Bible in moments of despair or heartaches, she found that devotionals, which included scriptures, inspired her and gave her the encouragement to keep moving forward. Her heart is to encourage those around her who may just need a glimpse of hope in this dark world by allowing the light of Jesus to shine through her. She hopes each reader knows that they are never alone in their journey.